THE NINE GRADATIONS OF LIGHT

THE NINE GRADATIONS OF LIGHT

Joseph Zaccardi

Bark for Me

狗

PUBLICATIONS

Fairfax, California

ISBN: 978-0-9762478-2-1
Book design, and cover art, *Prophesy*, by Jeremy Thornton, jftdesign.com

Bark for Me

狗

PUBLICATIONS

The Nine Gradations of Light
Joseph Zaccardi

Poems

Table of Contents

Introduction

BRIGHTNESS

GRAYNESS

DARKNESS

Introduction

Joseph Zaccardi writes about what is relevant to all of us — death, and therefore life; desire, time, distance, myth versus fact, war and its consequences.

The Nine Gradations of Light is a gift, a lyrical journey into how people have dealt with these connections through the ages. The words have authority in the palpable images and in the multiple meanings they convey.

His poems come from the heart, with a purity that comes from truth. They hold paradox, and a belief that takes the reader inward towards his or her own self. Joe has taken me to places I have never been before.

This collection is divided into three sections: "Brightness," "Grayness," and "Darkness." The poems themselves easily move between these "...Gradations of Light," but what I came to realize is that brightness could just as well cause blindness, or grayness could sharpen the mind's focus and attentiveness to detail as in "Standing in the Mudflats," where "the very distant / a breath away," reminds us to appreciate our pleasures, and that darkness, by its very contrast to any light, could uncover the nearly imperceptible, as in the poem "Disappearance," where he cautions us, "We disappear, / we disappear. As soon as the smoke / is done. As soon as the worm / is done."

I'm drawn towards Joe's love of Classical Chinese poets: "A Wang Wei Poem" about the joy of the journey. In "Li Po and the Student," he writes, "Now, Li Po says to his student, take this poem / throw it into a stream and watch it sail away." And in the middle section, as well as on the back cover of the book, is the tender poem "Exile" about Su Tung-Po: "Last night there were little green lights / in the shacks I passed on my journey, tonight nothing."

In "Recipe" we learn how to make golabki, "Some people call it / pigs-in-a blanket. But that was after the Nazis and Stalin. Now / here's how to make the sauce, my secret: sour cream, / Hungarian paprika, and the fat from the pan juices, and flour. / Without this, they lie like unclothed bodies side by side." My family and I ate pigs-in-the blanket every other week or so when I was growing up, and though I no longer consume red meat, I couldn't possibly eat a pigs-in-blanket after reading this most poignant poem; it contains one of the most powerful images I've ever read.

In the heartbreaking and incantatory last poem, "Arroyo's Soul," it is a different kind of death in the living, when he writes, "An age of lies and double talk." "In place of hope, indifference." "In place of song, noise."

The Nine Gradations of Light is an elegant and extraordinary book about the soul and about transformation. I treasure Joe's voice, and the depth of his wisdom.

– **Stephanie Mendel**
    author of *March, before Spring*, and *Bare Branches*

BRIGHTNESS

The place he found beyond expression bright,
Compared with aught on Earth, metal or stone —
Not all parts like, but all alike informed
With radiant light, as glowing iron with fire.

from: *Paradise Lost,* Book III, lines 591–594, by John Milton

The Nine Gradations of Light

Firstly brightness,
which is given as ten to the power of ten,
and is given to mean miracles and snow blindness.
It tears at the eyes; it carries water into the thinness
between air and vacuum.

And is the closest thing to God, and is of itself in three parts.

Secondly grayness,
which is given as ten to the power of ten hundred,
and is given to mean the knowledge of a millennium
and shortsightedness.
It rends the brain; it clocks everything in its sameness.
It is as pliant as mercury, as malleable as iron.

And is always halfway between greatness and smallness,
and is of itself in three parts.

Thirdly darkness,
which is given as ten to the power of ten thousand,
and is given to mean eternity and the end of time.

It is without vision, without thought.
It is without voice, without sound.

And is the closest thing to nothingness,
and the sum of its three parts equals itself.

They are the absence, and the presence.
They are the void, and the amplitude.

Each Thing Separate and Not Separate

What the soul wants is spring, the body
wrapped around the soul wants peace. And the day
always looking for the opposite wants night
but has only flecks and particles.

The beginning. The end.

The day is always lacking.
What the soul wants is fire, and the body
burns white-hot and wants water.

What the soul has is silence.

And the body gathers in its own blood rush.

In night. In winter.

Two white swans on a black lake,
the Chinese poet wrote,
they touch the water

and the water touches them.

The Swimmer

Her body covered in water becomes buoyant when she reaches
displacement's counterpoint to gravity. When the hands part
the water, and fan from head to torso, an arc is made,
and there is movement — something alive. Water
beneath and above. The same light that strikes the earth
strikes the body, this body, and then she breaks out
into open air, to an emptiness, her form in her wake,
she strokes the water's surface as though it were another
body with needs.

The Body as Seen from a Distance

Watching you and the curve of your breasts.
Want can be synonymous with hurt, both exquisite
and bitter. Turning and turning can wear away.
Absence is not like having never been, not even
close to never was. I write this with your pen,
the one that fell between the sofa cushions
while the turn-table hissed because the record
had played out. What stares back from the mirror
becomes the self. A glasscutter scores the glass
to ensure a clean break; in this way it is
like memory or a story learned by heart
that changes over time. The way being held
and holding are not the same.

All Things Good and Bad

There is a part to regret that holds
both hands to the breastbone, an argument
against the self—and though many years
pass there is still doubt and blame, inside
and outside the soul and the body, demanding,
giving away—like the she-wolf trying
to cover up her own scat but unable to resist
turning in a circle to smell again the trace,
and in so doing leads the hunter
to her den—and the hunter, black-hearted,
kills her and her pups, who were always hungry,
who were pure as drops of blood
in snow.

Toward the End of Day

There are five white geese
searching the rushes of a tide pool,
as though something had been lost
and lay near. They wade in and out
the way hunger pangs come and pass,
the way life waits on the heart.
There's a cool offshore breeze.
And what was once empty fills.
Just as willow fluff covers this water
and these white geese fly off
carrying red veils.

Standing in the Mudflats

The tide low and the sun low.
Two cranes stretch their wings, dance around
by turns. The day backlit and fading.
And in this brief confluence, light
sharpens, renders them invisible,
with only sea sounds
from the very distant
a breath away.

Variations of Sound at Night

The way sound is remembered.
The way sound covers and uncovers.
How different these differences.
A dead end street. The way it turns
around on itself. Under a winter moon,
sadness and quietness. Wind and surcease.
Traffic coming and going. The wings
of the unseen. The fragility.
The way a knock on a door
three blocks away reverberates.
That sound, that oneness.

There Is Nothing and Nothing Is Vast

Do you think you are not a part of this
or that it is not sewn together? The mind,
the heart, the whole body, each organ in tune,
and the cells with their memory
and the breathing that goes on
when the brain shuts down and the demands
of the heart? Despair is unnecessary
to function. A dream is real
and exists because it is yours. It is a longing
that cannot be shared. The universe appears
and disappears and is called time.
The wave and its white curl, each branch
of a stream diminishes, each limb
leaves and takes its dimension
of absence. Everyone knows this.
Everyone knows what is unknowable.
How is it this can be said: There is a thread
that turns in the 10,000 lights.
Someone walks across a field through calf-high
yellow grass that flattens before him,
makes a path and returns.

To Be

To find water when there is drought,
to find dry shelter when there is flood,
to not wrestle with the wind but to be
a part of wind, to rest beneath the Bo tree
and watch the wolves watch the hares,
to read their prints in the dust, escape
and challenge, to know all the uses of fire,
understand the messages of clouds, study
a lifetime the ways of the sea, to be a part
and apart, to know and not know all things
are within reach. To touch, yes, to touch again.
To know nothing is against what passes
overhead at night, what floats between.
To sleep a long time, to waken.

Room Enough

With dreams, take them as they are.
With night, take a sliver and make a blanket.
With fear, keep it away from the heart.
Take courage into the body, into the mind.
With loneliness, make a home,
make up the bed, make room.
With love be wise, be content, squeeze love,
speak love, let love drip slowly like an answer
to a difficult question.
Stall.

The True Meaning of Love

A lion waits in his den for the heat of the day to dissipate.
Then goes at dusk to where he has wanted to go
all day: to the river to drink water from water, to look
at the way the land and the sky divide and fit together
perfectly. He decides to not bring down the lame wildebeest,
not because he is not hungry, but because he feels generous
and hopeful.

Myth & Truth

In the place where they were to meet, under
the mulberry. From these leaves is silk spun.
One tale from another and another. When Thisbe fled
from the lion, the lion took her scarf in his mouth
and the lamb's blood from his muzzle did spoil it,
and thereupon Pyramus thought his beloved slain
and fell upon his sword, and she upon returning
threw her body over his sword that did protrude
from his heart and she died also. And the mulberries
turned from white to red. Today, the lion paces
the savanna. He has heard the tales about this one
and that one disappearing. Everything returns and dies,
returns and dies. Today the evening, then tomorrow.
The waterhole retreats and fills again. He remembers.
There are days and days when he does not eat.
There are days and days when he does not make a sound.
One word for myth, one word for truth.
One for silkworm, one for lion.

Another Psalm

Upon the flesh of the living, a blessing.
On the outside, on the inside. Yes, give thanks,
say prayer, though the world will strip bare
all that is covered, one day turning upon the other,
the peeling away of each season.
These are the certainties: to seed and to harvest,
to tend and to consume. Want and life.
To realize upon the barren, upon the rock,
things will one day grow, become fertile,
and then drought and fire, then flood and silt.
Over and over. Give blessing, give blessing
upon the flesh. The distant spring, the coming summer.
The lives of all of us in this our life.

Want

I want to know the spirits are here,
want doors to open and close by themselves,
want to be spoken to and to speak back,
though being frightened by death, still
want to meet the departed, dearly or otherwise.
Haven't the heart to name those I miss most.
When I walk in the woods I want the smell of violets,
fallen leaves, the must of mushrooms, snow.
I want to visit a desert twice. Want all the pictures
on the packets of dried seeds in their white racks
at the hardware store to fulfill their promise.
I want to dance in moonlight, ghostlike,
to slaughter a lamb before a stone image.
I want a religion made of wind and clouds, fetishes
of wood. I want what the termite wants:
to devour.

Chrysanthemums

Some say what we live today is another's life.
So I wasn't too surprised that time when I first tried
chrysanthemum tea in a Chinese restaurant, when I lifted
the teapot lid, witnessing the full bloom steeping,
steam bringing its pungent odor into the open,
somehow familiar, in the way we sometimes recognize
someone who reminds us of another we once knew.
And what happens to the beautiful things of the earth
that feed the body and the shadow of the body,
substance of everything some call the soul, ever changing
shape, because things change direction and give new form
to the different and the alike. I rushed back to my flat
on Russian Hill to look up all the varieties of mums,
studied the pen and ink drawings of flowers in the margins,
and read the best time to plant, to prune, how far up
the stalk, the hours of sun needed, which are edible,
which bring the best luck, make the best tea,
and which to carry.

Plot and Scene

What is space but a place
waiting for a thought to fill it?
The way a movie director calls
for all the actors to fire blanks
into another actor, until everyone
gets their parts right, until everything
in the script is acted on.

Work and Figure

A man hammers a nail into a board on a deck he is building.
Two nails into the width of each board, into sixteen joists,
sixteen inches apart. He raises his hammer, he brings it down.
The flat head strikes the nail. He does this three times to each nail.
The air rings with this contact of metals. There are sparrows
in formation overhead. There are angels no one can see. In the air,
answers. The swing of the man's hammer. He miters
another board to fit in a corner of this deck.
The precise fit. Everything on the earth fits this way.
A man raises his hammer, brings it down upon a nail.
He is putting two things together.

Together

The way the grain in the wood meets
on a door frame. The mortise and tenon
of the six panels, the bottom and top rails,
the stiles on the sides, the jamb, the cutout
for the doorknob and locks. The way the grain
in wood meets a carpenter's left hand,
how he caresses for perfection. That hand
takes the splinter and finds its way into the palm,
the life line. And what does it take to extract
where that sliver meets the flesh, digs in?
The door pushed against that which cannot be held back.
Pain is always about the way in,
the way out.

Devouring Time

Think of silkworms and mulberry leaves.
Think of the middle ground, the common.
How the body betrays and foretells.

Tranquility to tranquility.

The ox, so beautiful, laden and yoked,
turns the millstone.
Spin goes the flywheel.

Everything metered and precise.

Surely there are those who tire of the counting,
and those who are tireless.
But the truth is, time is self-fulfilling.

Time is.

Time and Change

I don't believe in the future
because it comes too fast.
                    –Einstein.

In the earth is the past, alive

with the buried and the fossilized.

And always it is where the present comes from.

Coastlines replaced, and all that falls

into the roil reformed. The future always

on the outside, an aura called time.

Someone stands at shoreline holding

a stoppered bottle containing only words.

It is proverbial, part faith, part hope.

It is psalm, part prayer and demand. If found,

it is someone's fortune (Calvin called it our fate).

If lost, it is the world's loss (Milton's paradise).

The present is a religion made up

of those who believe in the past

and those who don't believe.

December, Hiking on the Switchback

The mountain trembles the way bear might
on its last day before hibernation. Or maybe
from the cascade of snow, or maybe from something
deeper in the earth; the way an old woman might
when she remembers something from long ago
about pain; she might shift to one side of her body
to relieve some pressure to the bone and take
a deep breath through her teeth and make the sound
reeds make when an offshore breeze comes
over the marsh and bends them, just enough to resist,
and the reeds might whistle and scratch
their edges together like sabers
at the end of a day, this day, sky red.

The Sea

To be the spirit inside the body. To pull against
and be with desire. To listen to the heart and listen
to the voice. How they repeat, helpless
to stop injury. To know deceit when you see it.
To wait for each return. To be the body that contains
the spirit. That which holds the reins.
To know that light is cast down as is rain.
To not look up with expectation. To know
that fire too is transition. To touch everything twice.
Once to know and once to remember.
To wait by the sea for no reason.

GRAYNESS

Now came still Evening on, and Twilight grey
Had in her sober livery all things clad;
Silence accomplished; for beast and bird,
They to their grassy couch, these to their nests
Were slunk, all but the wakeful nightingale.

from *Paradise Lost,* Book IV, lines 598–602, by John Milton

The Tools of the Heart and the Three Mountains

Of the first it is barren, with footings of fallen rock,
as though being devoured, being pushed upward.
And the sky is its dividing line, the surrounding plain
its dividing line.

The heart is a pickax in the earth, and is wistful.

Of the second it is verdant, and increases its girth and climb;
breathes in and out according to the time of day.
And the sky is its dividing line, the green tips
its dividing line.

The heart is a shovel in the earth and is called desire.

Of the third it is snow-covered and ice-sheared,
which both builds and sloughs its weight.
And the sky is its dividing line, light
its dividing line.

The heart is a wrench in the earth and is called longing.

Grand Canyon

Mistakes happen, and Sam said, shit happens.
He's talking about the trip he and Janet took
to the Grand Canyon. They drove from SF
in her taupe Lincoln, stayed at roadside motels
all the way they're rocking the bedsprings.
Oh sweet mystery of love, said Sam,
half-singing, half-torch-songing. We took our time,
three meals a day, picture taking at each
pullout with a view, had a room with hot tub
and HBO in Palm Springs, a two-day layover
in Vegas, dropped three bills. Spared no expense.
Arrived at the Canyon Lodge at sunset, stood
at the rim, one step from eternity. Fucking beautiful,
Sam said, and Janet never looked better.
I tell you, the altitude changes the brain, and I popped
the question, and she said, without missing a beat,
Sam, I like things the way they are. I can't marry you.

Let the air out my tires, I tell you. We drove back,
hardly spoke a half-dozen words, made one pit stop
at some Podunk town off of I-5, and when I dropped her
off at her place in the Presidio, she said, Sam, I'll call you,
and I said, you do that. Mistakes happen,
that's okay, but shit is something you step in,
without warning.

Rarities

What is rare cannot be seen
without effort. Cannot be heard
or touched without regret. Because
it is the nearly lost, the nearly gone.
In some ways it is like the shark
that stays where the water is darkest
and preys upon what it alone can see.
This is the way with the rare.
A white deer. A white-headed crow.
One a symbol of long life, the other of death.
It is difficult to tell why an absence
of color should determine the fate
of one over the other.

A Wang Wei Poem

You finally understand this poem
you say you've been taken with.
You say it is not about the stone
thrown into the lake, not about the sound
or the wetness or the depth,
or decreasing light, and heavens no,
it's not about the ripples, not even
about the density of stone and water
or this joining that is not a joining.
You say it is about the intricate radiance
of this thought, not the measure of the impact
but what it imparts. You say this
while we are riding in the last seat
on a passenger train taking us
somewhere, just taking us.

Li Po and the Student

He unfurls a scroll of rice paper, snatches up a brush,
dips it into fresh ink, scrawls seven characters.
His student throws a handful of sand over the wet
surface of the poem, blows off the loose grains,
reads aloud, then looks up and around at the way
the red delta stretches flat, how a lone boatman stands
in the stern swaying an oar twice his height,
how three herons touch their wings to water
and dragonflies hover in the rushes,
how a stickwalker practices among the brown
humpbacks of water bison, and beyond,
a circle of huts in the haze of wood smoke.
Now, Li Po says to his student, take this poem,
throw it into a stream, and watch it sail away.

Rearranging Paths

A boy is practicing to be a stickwalker.
He has learned the first lesson. Each step
demands another. How far must he go
to feel confident enough to stop looking
down? As we walk in one life, the space
between the next life diminishes, his mother told him.
He is now ten-feet tall, eye level to a branch
on a peach tree. And ants hurry along,
hungry and content in their work, carrying
the sweet jelly they've collected back
to their underground home. That the boy
who has grown so and has bumped his head
and fallen is of little concern to them.
It is a mistake to think that what the body feels
is any different from what the soul feels.
Just because one life is reborn and another
leaves is not a coincidence.

Parable of the Mountain and the Birds

The mountain sits in dominance
over the valley, alone.
It too was once flat land, prairie.

The rivulets and streams sing this tale.

The mountain replies,
This is only echo and rumor.

Great pines dig into its body,
to find the cold water deep in, grow tall
to midriff, nearly to shoulder.

Birds rise and perch, chattering

about life
in the lowlands, where food
and seed are more abundant.

The mountain begins to wear down,
the way a man grows bald
from too much thinking.

Exile

Su Tung-Po squats in the belly of his skiff.
He makes an entry in his journal: *Windless,*
the hanging trees along the banks motionless,
a subtle current moves me farther south.
Last night there were little green lights
in the shacks I passed on my journey, tonight nothing.
I think of the great poets who have come before
and those who will follow.

Nine Ways of Seeing

Through haze gathered around the body
of the earth. Through moist eyes, through
the gaze of sighs. Through silence. Through sea
sounds made before a storm. Through
the moans of two entwined. Through shadow.
Through a lifetime. To watch two people
watch the setting.
And in the two of them,
the nine ways.

The Rule of Kings

The emperor is alone.
In the throne room he sits motionless.
When you have lost something it is better
not to turn around, not to ask where is it.
He calls out for jasmine tea. His speech is slurred.
Command what you want, he remembers
his third mother telling him when he was a boy.
And you must not touch what you desire.
The tea is held out to him, in a red bowl,
by a servant. He is on his knees,
eyes looking down. *Do not move
until you're certain,* she said, *do not ask
what others wish for.* Wise counsel
for both servant and emperor.
She smiled. *What have you lost?*
*The tea is cold. Still you should blow on
the surface to cool it further.*

Another History

The emperor is on the palace steps,
he is wearing the regalia of a warrior,
resplendent in gold and jade, and secretly
wishes to put an end to all fighting.
It is a thought that frightens him.
And the empress, he does love her, or did.
Because he has not touched her for a year
she now shies away from him, stays in
the shadows of the court and has taken
to spending her evenings with her eunuch,
who if the rumors are true is much endowed.
He plucks his facial hair and eyebrows
to hide his true nature. She weeps for her past.
The emperor has many concubines
to choose from. What is there to explain?
There is pain in joy and joy in pain.
And forgiveness. What is that but a slow poison?
And what is a tear but a bargaining chip?
So potent, all the perfume in the sixteen kingdoms
cannot disguise it.

Another History II

Eight times the emperor ordered his army
to drive out the barbarians who had settled on his lands in the north.
Each spring the barbarians would return with their tents and oxen.
The ninth time he had his army cut out the hearts of these trespassers.
His troops carried the severed hearts in sacks through the blue-lotus gates
into the heart of the city. Division, said the Chinese mathematician,
is the deconstruction of pure science. He explained further:
If you cut the head of an enemy off, the heart continues
to beat, for a time, without any thought, but when you cut
out the heart, everyone understands the uselessness.
The body dies from separation,
from not having.

The Glare

What sleeps beyond the mountain
we do not know, we hear only the rumble.
Call it thunder, call it drums. It is everywhere.
And in the interval the air is static, the sky
lower when a flash seems to rise from the valley.
Call it natural, heat compressing. Say it is
the emptying of cannons, say it is five-hundred-
pound bombs dropped, homes and bridges
beyond the mountain turned into red lanterns.
Who watches the weather? Who watches the war?

The Other Price of War

After the emperor and the emperor's soldiers left
the walled city. After the dust from their horses
had settled. The great black-lacquered doors closed.
The heavy wooden bar was slid into place.
The rest of the day was spent, for those left behind,
folding and unfolding hands. They watched
the gut-red sun disappear. They felt bereft without
the day, without the mountains to look upon.
And in the back of their minds was the thought
of the one forgotten gate left unsecured.
To find a path, all doubt must do is wait.

Warnings, Predictions, and Admonitions
to the Empress Wu from the Minister of Rites

If you find a white stone, you will be elevated.
If in a bowl of water a blue lotus appears to you,
your reign will be long. If the day is bitter cold
and you can still love, you will have many sons
and many daughters. If you wake to a sky
in another place and there is a bridge over silver water,
a spell has been cast upon you. If, however,
you see bluebirds, it is a message from the goddesses
that the spell has been thwarted.
A white-headed crow is always a bad omen.
Celebrate the ninth day of the ninth moon
and the third day of the third moon, autumn and spring,
to insure prosperity. Remember the morning glory
opens with the sun and fades with the day.
White butterflies turn yellow in winter.
Do not live by the waters of the Huang Ho. Weigh the facts
but heed the texture of someone's testaments.
Even a mute knows the ten thousand words.
Truth can be found in the eyes and in the hands.

Father

The wizard casts a spell over his children.
He tells them of the dark green forest
and the house made of gingerbread,
then he says *Sleep now,* says their names
over and over. His voice is musical, his voice beautiful.
He turns off the light and chants: *yellow bells,*
stone chimes, moon guitars and red drums,
bamboo flutes carved with phoenix wings
and dragon heads.

Distance Is a Tyranny

It's in the way a river holds to its bank
only to diminish.

Forget about overflows and droughts.
Silent, dusky light clings like cloth to the body.
In every good Chinese poem a peach is mentioned.

In every flux and effluence a feather in the current.
A dim lantern figures the trees around the darkened huts.

What is buried in the earth is cold and what hurries empties,
the way sand keeps at beach glass.

True prayer is wordless.
And nothing,
nothing is ever too far.

Gait

That the horse died in her tracks beneath the man
she'd carried all those years, meant he'd have to walk
the rest of the way. Together they had covered a lot
of ground. The man thought that he was nearer to where
he'd end up than to where he'd lit out from. When the horse was alive
he would sometimes talk to her and she would listen and think
about his voice. Now as he walks alone he talks to himself,
not always in agreement as to what he is saying.
There are many more miles to walk yet and some steep
inclines ahead, some marshes where the muck will suck
at his boots and some sand where he'll sometimes feel
he is losing ground. But by and by, he will get to where
he is headed for — a place where the last of his words
will catch up with the last of his thoughts about the horse
who died in her tracks and didn't care to know
where they were going.

To Uncover

Deceit lies in desire.
In lust, some truth.
Happiness yearns for loss.

In every request, blackmail
and in sadness some trickery.
In touch, some want.
A kiss implies obligation.

In every handshake, flattery and envy.

There is in jealousy some grief.
        In every garden, a fruit
that is bitter.
        In every garden, a root
that grows from another's yard.

DARKNESS

The Prince of Darkness speaking to the Son of God:

In what degree or meaning thou art called
The Son of God, which bears no single sense.
The Son of God I also am, or was;
And, if I was, I am; relation stands:
All men are the Sons of God...

from *Paradise Regained,* Book IV, lines 516–520, by John Milton

What It Is to Feel and to Not Feel

What you know is what you want to hear.
What you can't hear: something stalking in the forest
with bared teeth, radiation, healing, people
locked away for no good,
light changing, color.

What you watch is what you want to see.
What you can't see: around the bend,
a bullet after it has left the chamber, God.
A child behind closed doors.
Black and blue under a cloak.

What you feel is what you want to touch.
What you can't touch: death, nothing,
someone's hate. What a vulture feels
eating the entrails of a doe. That color
of red.

What you think is what you want to speak.
What you can't speak: the truth
all the time about what matters,
the name of anything you cannot
hear or see or touch. The reason

gray darkens light and lightens dark.

An Act of Patience

There is a song the scarlet ibis sing
in their trees at the start of evening
when the god-clouds redden, in the season
of mating. It is a song without one hurried note,
and in another tree there is another and another song.
The birds dip their heads as one might at a party,
unappeased by the conversation alone, yet unwilling
to leave, unwilling to be unloved.

Song of the Dispossessed

For we are small.
We must blend into the rushes,
bend with wind.
Our eyes, dull, monochromatic,
must not reflect.
If punched in the belly
we'll not respond.
If whacked on the kneecap
we'll not reflex.

We must deflect.
In sun we must not squint,
nor shall we look directly.
Under the moon
we must not resist the pull.
If the tide is out we are adrift.
If the tide is in we are awash.
If a part of the sea, we must be krill
to the whale, chum to the shark.

When expelled, we float or sink.
If we breathe, we drown.
If beached, we dry in the sere.
The salt will pinch and parch.

If consumed on land we must pass
over the muzzle, through the gullet.
We must not flinch.

If found, we must lie still.
If we are burned, we rise
in the ether and disperse.

We must be unseen
as the wind is unseen.
In the rushes we are without need,
for we are small,
and without words.

Recipe

Parts of the skillet:
the hanging ring, the handle and tang, the iron side and bottom,
the seasoned surface, the weight.

She's showing me how to make golabki — she says the word
slowly, go-om-pkee, so I'll understand — how to scald the cabbage,
how much rice to cook up, the pinches of salt and the measure
of thyme, what cuts of pork and beef are best, what attachment
to use on the meat grinder that has the raised foundry's name
under the lip of the hopper.

What's golabki mean, I ask, I mean literally.

Parts of the knife:
the rivets on the handle, the bolster, guard and heel,
the back of the blade, the blade, the free edge, the point.

Golabki means golabki, she says. She sniffs. Some people call it
pigs-in-a-blanket. But that was after the Nazis and Stalin. Now
here's how to make the sauce, my secret: sour cream,
Hungarian paprika, and the fat from the pan juices, and flour.

Without this, they lie like unclothed bodies side by side.

A Lived Life

Every day ends. Dirt thrown into an open
space to hold more than was taken out.
Are you coming? Are you coming?
Words spoken in passing. Always
seeking, always changing, always
into nothing. Everyone brings flowers,
they bring them and plant them and then
the bulbs go to sleep, wait until the longer days
come and then grow towards light.

A List of Names

Everything passes over their heads,
just as everyone passed before them.
And their foreheads flower with worms.
Everything is nourished in its own time.
And everyone has trouble with the hours.
Without a picture there is no face. Without
a body, the name given is unknowable.
History moves on to the next war and to the next.
The day's task is always the same; nothing hurries it.
That is why the hour is familiar and unfamiliar.
And the list of names doesn't bother
with the elements, doesn't notice the cold,
doesn't notice the heat. And the list
of names no longer hungers or desires.
It is a just list, Malraux thought,
and fate leads us to our inevitable defeat.

Truth & Immortality

Everyone leaves things behind, the solids
and the dreams. Gardens grow red.
Fruit ripens and falls. The great books
all say the same thing, Even you.
A farmer unearths a stone in the tilling.
A wanderer makes a map of where
he's been and plans the next trip.
No one is ever truly lost. Truth is more
difficult to find than a buried stone,
or what a journey has in store.

Disappearance

We too shall disappear to where you are.
If heaven be in the clouds.
If heaven be in the ancient stars.
All our lived lives patched together.
Each strand crossed over and under.
No one recognizable from any other.
We too shall disappear to where you are.
If heaven be a part of the earth's soil.
If heaven be a part of rock, molten rock.
All the buried lives consumed
and broken down. Solidified,
hardened, petrified. History
and the forgotten. Days and nights
the same. Be still, you dead. Be silent.
We too shall disappear to where you are.
Become unrecognizable. We disappear,
we disappear. As soon as the smoke
is done. As soon as the worm
is done.

Again April

The spirit is gone. And the people
who wore it before are gone.
These two things taken together
are absence: the fruit and the seed.
One cannot live without the other.
And though the memory of either
is often described, it cannot spring back.
It is as if someone tried to tell you
everything there is to know
about the death of the month of April
or an abyss or the taste of a dark fruit.

The Tunic

What is a part of the body is a part of the earth,
like the tuber, the bulb waiting for the heat to permeate,
the amount of rain needed. Until then the deep freeze
or terrible storm is of the ether, the future, on the outside.
What is part of the body is a part of the hunger. It is not
the menu, the careful choices. It is the preparation,
the taking in, the taste, the settling of the craving
at the dinner hour. What is a part of the body
is a part of time, the expected and predicted,
the day to day, one season pulling the rug out
from under the other, not the absurd, the blind alley,
the dead end. What is a part of the body is like nothing
else: neither light nor lack, nor the sky's height
nor gravity's weight. The universe blinks in and out.
In that way it is like the body.

Only Words

Swallow your words. Plunge headlong
into water. Even there you can hear
laughter. Go under, go under.
Even though someone is speechless
does not mean he does not cry out.
Close your eyes, and still you can see.
The light comes through, the dark
comes through. Words are simple
and not so simple. They can be used
with understanding and not.
Turn nothing over
and what have you?

Great Deluge

Nature cannot determine what it repeats.
A stone on the bottom of a river becomes
a dream, water transparent as glass holds
the solid in amplification — wearing and honing
the hard with the soft. Take a bucket of seawater
from one ocean and empty it into another ocean.
Each is refilled. Ballast carries its own weight.
The destiny of everyone is to become stone,
a compact with the earth. And the rains
and the floods make everything
equal.

A Way to Hold Someone

Almost a dance whose steps reconfigure,
learning hand to hand, the bodies entwine.
Even if unequally matched — different weight,
different height — there is always something
in the other, so that the weaker can gain
advantage, not unlike David of the slingshot
and the giant taking it in the head.
And when one man takes another down,
how it feels holding him almost tenderly
but firmly in practice, so no further harm
can come, a test of whether one has
what it takes to wrestle an enemy
for real, till he is still as water.

Gravity

To escape gravity is to stand still.
The earth trading one place for another.
And the flying things above would keep
to their compasses; both the man-made
cold metal and the hollow-boned and feathered.
If this could be done — a human with the mind to,
with just the body in the airless — time would
stop for them: the watch static, unhurried.
The end would become more distant.
Is this not what is hoped for? Is this not
what everyone talks about, the voiding
of death, life bargained away for eternity?

I Know That I Know Nothing

–Socrates

There is one language
and there are many languages.
And the hands and the deeds
of hands are translations.
There are questions
in everyone's eyes,
and answers are the lines
between day and night,
something to put a word on,
to put many words on.
The ocean extinguishes the sun
and the other way around.
If there were no longer a universe
would the last word be *no?*
One word, all words.
The hand and the deed.
Many hopes, many hopes.
Belief in nothing
means it is impossible to know.
Belief means to know that nothing
does not exist.

Timepiece

Everything is a big thing. Always more
could be said about the size, and the path.
Is there any point to eternity? A beginning
with no ending. In so many ways
an hour holds the answer: it says
you've run out of time, and then
starts over again.

The Nearness of Oblivion

Thoughts fold the way a wave enfolds
the body, revising past things in the mind
to find the most allowable position,
the most comfortable. Qualifying, always qualifying.
Soon summer descends, the humidity bearable,
the fireflies restless small suns going in and out.
And there was a glass bowl of fresh peaches
cooling in ice water. Not a blemish anywhere,
no signs or indication
of oblivion.

Skimming Stone

Someone said there are holes in the universe,
a vortex where light bends and collapses.
Where there is no escape. And today
there is a fog that is stubborn, thick
as the proverbial, so much so even geese
have stopped flying low over Alpine Lake.
It's as though the world were upside down,
white-clouded, nebulous.

Someone tosses a stone, something hard entering
the pliant, bottoming out. To leave this world
means to have a permanence most wouldn't
want, at least not right now, not knowing
in which end of the sky they'll find themselves
or how many steps to the precipice or how far down.
If you have to go.

The Daily Order

The sun rises.
To be more exact, the earth rotates and orbits.
People wake and leave their warm beds.
People who are ill and tired
contemplate and recollect.
And the prophets sit up and cross their legs.
And all, in their own way, seek
the unequivocal answers, ask
the unanswerable questions.

The sun sets.
The earth turns away.
The sun returns to the same things
it has so recently left. It is different
and not different. The sun warms and cools,
wakens and eases. Without memory,
without mind, it stays on the meridian.

Not yet and not then.
And everyone takes a hand
in the day.

Withdrawn

A man draws a map.
He points his finger here and here,
says this is mine and this valley is mine,
the river that runs between is mine.
I will take this mountain and all the trees
that grow upon its sides, the shattered rocks
near the base I will take, this snow at the crest
like dust on a desktop I will take. And the wind
will be mine, and the wings of birds, the bees
that carry honey to their hives will be mine.
As for you, I give a desert, the annual rainfall
of three inches will be yours. Now if something
should be discovered beneath this sand,
this useless sand, I will draw new lines,
and explain to you again, because I have nothing
to hide. Nothing on this map
I draw every day is worthless.

One Source

There's a sweet potato half in, half out of a jelly jar,
on a kitchen window sill, in water. Four toothpicks stick
into the sides of its belly to hold one half in and one half out.
A kind of voodoo, a kind of rebirth, where the vine grows out
from the tuber, glossy-leaved, trailing. And on the other side
of a smeary half dormer there's a garden in decline, untended,
drying in a kind of last gasp, in drought, holding out for late rains
or the kindness of some tenant, a renter by the week of a studio
or an efficiency apartment, who'll turn on the sprinkler system
for maybe an hour, someone who might have a green thumb,
someone whose ancestors were farmers maybe, maybe the same
kind-hearted soul who plunked the sweet potato in the jelly jar,
a large jar from one of those warehouse stores that sell mayo
by the gallon and beef by the side, a discounter who sells in bulk
to people who want to save big and to those who find another use
for food, a return on their return — that yam-like pumpkin-colored spud,
that rootstock, starchy and calorie jam-packed. The one with the African
slave name from Haiti, a new-world food — something cheap, easy
to grow and store, and forgiving.

One Hand Washes the Other

–San Francisco

He shows me the tracks. The arm the way it is.
What would God say about what is done to the body?
He says he's fallen on hard times since he was rear-ended
at a stop sign, his chopper totaled, hog gone to the dump,
but he's getting clean, getting straight. He shows me
the scar on his back, the old tattoo
over his heart, half scraped away. It's the day
before Thanksgiving, and he needs forty bucks
to get to Sacramento, his family. But twenty will do,
he says, if that's all I have — he could hitch part way,
bus-it part way. He backs up, looks sideways, down.
I hand over the forty.

At Prego's, I have a nine-dollar martini with a twist —
think how nervous he seemed, how his teeth
looked bad, and his hands, and how we shook
on it, this deal, a short loan, how I was glad
to see him go, and the last look he gave me, quick
freeze. Now the smell of this gin, medicinal,
this cold alcohol. And the needle he'll use,
the shame of it.

Desert

Along an isolated road, a cactus dressed
in a cowboy outfit: hat, vest, low-slung holster. The eyes
and mouth, gouged-out holes, have turned black. Shape
of the living in the dying. It is said the ancient Egyptians
believed the essence of a being was in the heart, the body
a vehicle to the other side. The brain pulled through the nostrils
with a hook, discarded. The heart flows beyond form, petrifies
in the drying. The burning of a shooting star, one light
into another. Eden in darkness. Desert in full bloom.

Everything Is What It Seems

This is why you are here.
When something is planned
it is called an event.
When something happens
it is called happenstance.
I want to tell you how exquisite
your hair smells, you, who take me
in your arms. I want to tell you
my tears are from an old wound,
what the circumstance was and why.
You, whose eyes are half-closed,
you, who say nothing, who draw
your body to mine and say nothing.

Desperate Wishes

At the center of the earth is a molten core
of iron and nickel. Don't touch this, the gods say.
There are wounds deeper than you can imagine.
And the heart has separate chambers for a reason.
One for disappointment, one that can never be filled.

They tell us but we don't listen. We try to capture
the blue of the blue sea in jars, but it is always murky
and littered. We trap nine fireflies at dusk,
and in the morning all the light in them is gone.
We let them go, we pour them out.

Do you think
you are *you* for no reason? Do you know there are two
other chambers? If you put your ear to the heart,
any heart, it will say, *Do this and do this.* And the sky
will bleed out at the end of every day.

Arroyo's Soul

The river of ritual is parched.
Where once currents were deep and swift
is now a bed of dry stone.
Where once mendicants came,
in their place is a commemorative plaque.
Where once priests and shamans chanted,
now the curious come in search of the arcane.
Where once smoke from a volcano was seen
as a sign, now geologists explain.
There is no more honey-thick blood
to anoint the body of the novice.
All has been reduced to commentary.
It is an age of reason and cause.
An age of lies and double-talk.
Nothing can touch us. We are safe.
In place of incantation there is silence.
In place of protest, acquiescence.
In place of faith, acceptance.
In place of hope, indifference.
In place of song, noise.
The river no longer flows,
but we are waiting.

Notes

"Warnings, Predictions, and Admonitions to the Empress Wu from the Minister of Rites"

The Empress Wu Zetian was the only female in Chinese history to rule as emperor, even though according to Confucian beliefs having a woman rule would be as unnatural as having a "hen crow like a rooster at daybreak." During the most glorious years of the Tang dynasty, she did rule, and ruled successfully in one of China's more peaceful and culturally diverse periods.

"Li Po and the Student"

Li Po, (701 – 762), is regarded as one of the greatest poets of the Tang dynasty, often called China's "golden age" of classical Chinese poetry, he was both a prolific and a creative poet, as well as one who stretched the rules of versification of his time. According to many historical sources, it was a practice of Li Po to send his poems out on streams.

"Exile"

Born in 1036, Su Tung-Po was a famous Chinese poet; the journal entry of the poem in this collection is imaginary. His satiric verses and opposition to official policies frequently lost him his official status and resulted in imprisonment and twelve-times exiled. As an old man, he was banished to Hainan Island in the South China Sea; though pardoned he did not make it back to court and died on the trip north.

"Distance is a Tyranny"

The line, "In every good Chinese poem a peach is mentioned," is a quote from Li Po.

"Recipe"

In this poem "Pigs-in-a-blanket," in regions heavily influenced by Slovak immigrants, such as northern Pennsylvania and northeastern Ohio, usually refers to stuffed cabbage rolls, such as the Polish or Ukrainian golabki.

Acknowledgments

Grateful acknowledgment is given to the editors of the following publications in which these poems originally appeared.

Hunger and Thirst: Food Literature: "Recipe."

Medusa's Kitchen: "I Know That I Know Nothing," and "Exile."

Marin Poetry Center Anthology: "Withdrawn," "The Sea," "The Tools of the Heart and the Three Mountains," and "Gait."

Paterson Literary Review: "One Hand Washes the Other."

About the Author

Joseph Zaccardi is the author of two books of poetry, *Vents* (2005), and *Render* (Poetic Matrix Press, 2009). His poems have appeared in the *Southern Poetry Review, Runes, Poet Lore, Seattle Review, Spillway* and elsewhere. He volunteers at convalescent hospitals reading poetry to the residents, and listens to them recite the poems they know by heart.

Poetry came alive for Zaccardi in the 6th grade, when his teacher, Sister Francesca, gave him a small book of poems by William Carlos Williams; a gift, alas, that he has lost track of. Perhaps the power of poetry is that it stays with you, he says, even when it is not with you.

Born in Newark, New Jersey, on Labor Day, as a youngster, Zaccardi thought that that holiday was to commemorate his mother's labor while giving birth to him. He has been drawn to poetry because he believes that every poem has multiple meanings, in some ways, every new poem is like a newborn child.

Colophon

The typeface for the poems in this book is Garamond, the name given to a group of old-style serif typefaces named after the punch-cutter Claude Garamond (c. 1480–1561). He came to prominence in the 1540s, first for a Greek typeface he was commissioned to create for the French king, Francis I. The French court later adopted Garamond's Roman types for their printing, and the typeface influenced type across France and Western Europe.

Garamond's letterforms convey a sense of fluidity and consistency. He did however have flights of fancy with the italicized Q, W, and the ampersand, $\&$, where he allowed himself to head off from type to art. Garamond has also been noted to be one of the most eco-friendly major fonts when it comes to ink usage.